GOALS

ISBN 978-1-60810-050-7

www.simpletruths.com
Toll Free 800-900-3427

Book Design: Vieceli Design Company,
West Dundee, Illinois

Editing by Stephanie Trannel

PHOTO CREDITS:
Images courtesy iStockphoto.com

To those brave souls
who have the courage to
pursue their greatest dreams,
I dedicate this book to you!

THE DEFINITION OF A
GOAL

A goal is a specific, measurable,
and time-bound end toward
which you direct specific effort
until achieved!

TABLE OF CONTENTS

INTRODUCTION

Dear Friend,

On everyone's short list of things to do during their lifetime are the accomplishment of worthy goals and the fulfillment of one's purpose.

Achieving a goal is like opening a combination lock. You need the correct numbers in the correct right, left, right sequence. There are thousands of possible combinations; and if you are aware of the settings but not the sequence, your efforts will prove futile.

The Ten Rules of Goal Setting is the combination that opens the lock of success. *Each rule is one piece of the combination; each seamlessly integrates with the other nine; each one counts!*

This book provides the goal setting information you need in a straightforward and systematic manner. You will be hard pressed to find a goal that does not require each of these ten rules.

Not all goals are equal, but all goals contain the same foundational elements.

When it comes to setting goals, we often don't know what we don't know.

And, what you don't know can—and most likely will—hurt you by limiting or compromising your success.

Each rule calls for and requires know-how of multiple disciplines. No one is born with all the talents to achieve a goal—you learn as you go on the fly!

Everyone needs to know how to set and achieve a goal. Everyone needs an awareness of proportion and a keen sense of the possible. Everyone needs the will to pursue his or her dreams and to know what it takes to taste victory.

If I could carve ten rules for achieving a goal into the walls of your mind, they would be the ones contained in this book. The ten rules work because they are simple, and they are simple because they work.

The potential for personal growth and personal expression—as well as for mind-boggling personal wealth—makes this a time of opportunity … a time to create the kind of life that previous generations could not imagine. That is why goal setting is important.

Success is individual. Your definition of "the good life" may be very different from others'. Yet the underlying steps toward that end are the same. That similarity helps you to understand what success really is.

Success is the ability, first, to recognize opportunity; second, to form plans and strategies that leverage opportunity; and, third, to develop the necessary skills needed to execute those strategies.

The ten rules, like anything else in life, operate best if they are self-enforced!

Success is beautiful because of how it looks to you, how it works, how it feels, and how it represents the fulfillment of goals pursued. Grow accustomed to prosperity and confident in the process of achieving a goal. Embrace these ten rules of goal setting and give witness to a powerful transition in your life.

My goal is simply to help you achieve yours by teaching you the correct combination and correct sequence.

Gary Ryan Blair

Gary Ryan Blair
The Goals Guy

#1

BE
DECISIVE

Success is the intentional, pre-meditated use of choice and decision. Unless you choose—with certainty—what it is you want, you accept table scraps by default!

THE WORLD IS PLUMP WITH OPPORTUNITY.

With boldness and conviction, stick a fork into the goals you want by being decisive.

You are born with great capabilities, but you will not achieve your potential until you call upon yourself to fulfill it. You will rise to the occasion when it presents itself; yet, to assure self-fulfillment, you must provide occasions to rise to. Clearly defined goals allow you to travel toward another horizon that represents the end of one experience and the transition to a new and better existence. The objective is to choose the right goals, and then to create the necessary causes—the effects will follow!

> The DIFFERENCE between what one person and another achieves depends more on goal CHOICES than on ABILITIES.

The profound differences between successful people and others are the goals they choose to pursue. Individuals with similar talents, intelligence, and abilities will achieve different results because they select and pursue different goals.

EACH DECISION AFFECTS WHAT YOU BECOME. WE FORM OUR DECISIONS AND OUR DECISIONS FORM US.

There is no escaping this; the smallest choices are important because—over time—their cumulative effect is enormous.

Never overlook the obvious: The nature and direction of your life change the instant you decide what goals you want to pursue.

Once you make a decision, you start down a path to a new destination. At the moment the decision is made, your decision to pursue a goal alters what you are becoming. Just one spin of the lock's dial—a single choice—can alter your life, your destiny, your legacy.

Think about it—your goal decisions represent and express your individuality. You seal your fate with the choices you make.

YOU DEFINE YOURSELF BY YOUR DECISIONS.

Your dialog with success is ultimately a solo one. Decisions and goals made must be your own if you are to call your life a success.

Always establish the best goals you can. Goals are the seeds of success—you become only what you plant. The quality of your harvest is a direct reflection of the quality of your seeds ... your decisions!

Indecision is the big eraser of opportunity and potential. Risks and costs accompany every decision; however, the price of decision is far less than the long-range risks and costs of comfortable in-

TO ACCOMPLISH GREAT THINGS, WE MUST NOT ONLY ACT, BUT ALSO DREAM; NOT ONLY PLAN, BUT ALSO BELIEVE.

—Anatole France

action. When it comes to decisiveness, squatters have no rights.

Everyone has an official wish list of things they think are "reasonable." What about the unofficial wish list? The one that common sense tells you to ignore? The list that exists deep in your mind, the list that keeps you up at night, the list that makes your toes wiggle when you think of it? Why not choose that list for a change?

How long have you dreamed of being, having, and doing what you really want? Think big, as when it comes to your goals, the size of your ambition does matter.

A DECISION IS NEVER MADE ONLY ONCE.

A decision to lose weight and keep it off must be remade every time you feel hungry. To fully appreciate this insight you must snuggle up next to **RULE #2 ... STAY FOCUSED!**

#2

STAY FOCUSED

FOCUS = FOLLOW ONE COURSE UNTIL SUCCESSFUL!

Focus is the glue that holds a goal in place ... an insurance policy on your journey to success. If you've got a great goal or idea but not focus, you really don't have much.

WHAT EXACTLY IS FOCUS? Focus is simply a goal, a picture in your mind's eye of something you want. Your focus is usually spelled in CAPITAL LETTERS!

Focus is the equivalent of Moby Dick in a goldfish bowl … just too powerful to ignore.

A successful focus is based on the concept of singularity. Your goal must create in your mind both the perception and reality of importance.

THE MOST IMPORTANT ASPECT OF FOCUS IS
SINGLE-MINDEDNESS.

Because everything you do moves you closer to or further from your goal, focus cannot be considered in isolation. If everything you think, say, and do moves you toward your goal, then everything requires focus!

FOCUS CREATES A POWERFUL FORCE:
GOAL POWER.

The moment you focus on a goal, your goal becomes a magnet, pulling you and your resources toward it. The more focused your energies, the more power you generate.

There is a seismic shift in performance that takes place when you move from decisiveness to focus. The shift is caused, enhanced, and accelerated by the intensity of your focus. Focus is like plugging into a power source all its own.

If there are two goal setting elements that should be joined at the hip, no better pair exists than

DECISION AND FOCUS.

They feed off each other. Decision makes focus possible, and focus makes decision easier. Success offers living proof that decision and focus make for a lovely couple!

The moment you energize a goal with focus it will be as if the train you're riding instantly switches to a new set of tracks going in exactly the right direction at a high rate of speed.

We're all vulnerable—it is easy to lose focus. Accept the hard fact that you must repeatedly recover your focus. A brief loss of focus is a minor derailment, but, if not regained rapidly, loss of focus becomes a wholesale wreck. Focus, readjust, and realign— that's the recipe behind all great achievement.

EVERY OPPORTUNITY COMPETES FOR TIME AND FOCUS.

Resist temptation. You can't do everything, but you can do one thing and stay with it until completion.

Once you begin to focus, it's like telling the world, "Watch out ... here I come!" Focus signals the coming out of your goal.

Guard your focus jealously. Determine not to be distracted. Without focus, you lose your way ... enthusiasm disappears ... goals become faded aspirations. Goose your focus every day through constant care, feeding, and attention.

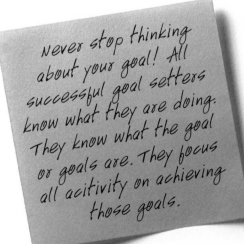

Never stop thinking about your goal! All successful goal setters know what they are doing. They know what the goal or goals are. They focus all acitivity on achieving those goals.

You will receive no sympathy in the marketplace for loss of focus. The feeding frenzy will begin the moment you allow your focus to wane. You put a bounty on your head every time you lose focus.

Focus requires that you get on top of your goals like a chicken on an egg!

Focus requires focus. Focus is a priority, a necessity, and an absolute; it practically guarantees a front-row seat to prosperity.

The power of focus lies in its ability to inspire purposeful action, but to leverage focus, you'll need a pen and a pad of paper because the next rule is **RULE #3 ... WRITE YOUR GOALS!**

SOME GIVE UP THEIR DREAMS WHEN THEY HAVE ALMOST REACHED THE GOAL; WHILE OTHERS, ON THE CONTRARY, OBTAIN A VICTORY BY EXERTING, AT THE LAST MOMENT, MORE VIGOROUS EFFORTS THAN EVER BEFORE.

— Herodotus

#3

WRITE
YOUR GOALS

Written goals are catalysts, transforming agents for success and achievement. Yet, like umbrellas and pens, unwritten goals almost always end in loss!

You will achieve far greater and more consistent results when you take the time to write down your goals. Writing goals sets off a chain of events that allows you and others to see and evaluate your goals so that you can develop plans to achieve them.

Goals kept only in your mind have an uncanny way of remaining figments of your imagination. The odds are against you ever acting upon them. *Goals not written down fall victim to the "out of sight ... out of mind" phenomenon!*

We've all had the experience of going to the supermarket with a "mental list" of stuff to get. Yet we inevitably return home without one or more desired items.

A simple written list would have been the perfect solution. Your goals work the same way, if you don't write them down, you will forget them.

ASK THE SIX IMPORTANT GOAL SETTING QUESTIONS

- **WHO** WILL BE INVOLVED IN HELPING YOU ACHIEVE THIS GOAL?
- **WHAT** IS THE GOAL? WHAT SPECIFICALLY DO YOU WANT TO ACCOMPLISH?
- **WHERE** ARE YOU NOW IN RELATION TO THIS GOAL?
- **WHEN** DO YOU EXPECT TO ACHIEVE THIS GOAL?
- **HOW** WILL YOU ACCOMPLISH THIS GOAL?
- **WHY** DO YOU WANT TO ACHIEVE THIS GOAL?

WRITING CHALLENGES THOUGHT. When you write a goal, you actually see what you're thinking. You have a target to aim for … something that takes shape and grows legs.

By writing your goals, you take a step toward achieving them. The writing process is an essential piece of the combination of achievement, a tremendous ally of focus.

From eureka to achievement, the evolution of a goal begins in the mind and immediately takes shape when pen is put to

Don't make the mistake of thinking you can keep your goals in your head. For goal setting to have any value, goals must be written down. Only by writing each step can you see where you are going.

paper. The goal progresses from thought to sketch, from sketch to action, and finally from action to achievement in real time.

THE ACHIEVEMENT OF A GOAL IS AN EXEMPLARY TALE OF POWER, PURPOSE, AND POTENTIAL.

The process of writing and revising a goal forces you to make a commitment to yourself; once a goal is written, you've made an investment. And, as with any investment, you'll want to protect it and nurture its growth.

If you intend to take goal setting seriously, you must up the ante by writing down your goals and revising them continuously.

By choosing your goal and writing it down, you gain an edge. Most people simply respond to conditions rather than create conditions for a better life. While there is no magic pill or equation for success, one thing is sure: Those who fail to plan by not writing down their goals, by default, plan to fail.

While blessed with permanent memory, your mind is cursed with lousy recall. Even if the only paper in sight is a cocktail napkin, write down your goal in complete detail.

Your mind works, and you execute best, with precise instructions.

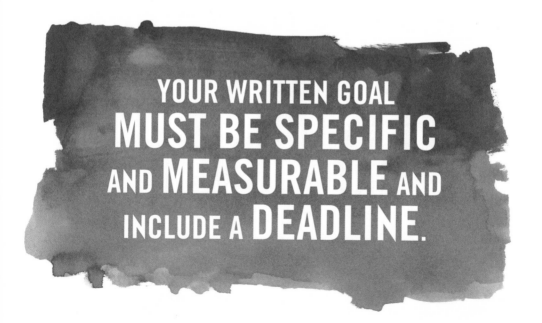

YOUR WRITTEN GOAL MUST BE SPECIFIC AND MEASURABLE AND INCLUDE A DEADLINE.

THE INDISPENSABLE FIRST STEP TO GETTING THE THINGS YOU WANT OUT OF LIFE IS THIS: DECIDE WHAT YOU WANT.

— Ben Stein

Your mind has a great capacity to think through facts, fiction, and circumstance to find ways to achieve your goals. What was once recorded on paper will soon be recorded in history ... as a goal achieved.

However, simply writing down your goal is not enough. Achievement requires the discipline that comes from **RULE #4** ... **PLAN THOROUGHLY!**

4

GOAL RULE # 4

PLAN THOROUGHLY

Here's the "deep dish" on planning: A well-defined plan properly executed is your meal ticket to success!

You can virtually guarantee your success in any endeavor if you know who you are, what you want, where you are going, how you will get there, and what you will do once you arrive.

Planning before taking action helps you to do things better, faster, and cheaper!

In addition to saving you 10 to 1 in execution, planning offers a host of other tasty benefits as well. Among the most important:

PLANNING...

PROMOTES FOCUS. It helps you visualize the promise of the future by cutting through clutter.

COORDINATES EFFORTS. It allows you to iron out the wrinkles in your goal. Planning serves as a catalyst for new insights and ideas.

PROVIDES STANDARDS. It helps you size up your performance and measure your progress. It provides a reality check on the good, the bad, and the ugly of achieving this goal.

PREPARES THE PLANNER. It gives you the tools you need to deal with sudden and unexpected problems.

REVEALS ROADBLOCKS. It gives you a clear picture of how different tasks and activities interact to ensure success. To be forewarned is to be forearmed.

STIMULATES THINKING. It leads you onward and upward by providing the stimulation you need to avoid dead-ends and blind alleys.

⮡ OFFERS AN EXIT PLAN. It gives you a sneak peek of what is expected and allows you to judge for yourself if the investment is worth the risk. It serves as an early warning system allowing you to bow out gracefully rather than be thrown out later on. A short time spent in planning can save you a long time of regret and misery.

Perfect the use of planning and you will win many battles by default. Planning means doing your homework … running twice as fast. A lawyer works out the opposition's legal arguments. An entrepreneur puts himself in the shoes of a contractual partner. The successful negotiator is the confident negotiator bolstered by advance knowledge and planning.

Substantive progress in reaching a goal is made through preparing—in private. If at all possible, sleep on plans that are extremely difficult. Resist the temptation to judge in a hurry. Patience and wisdom are virtues to be respected and honored.

Planning allows you to carefully orchestrate all the steps along the way to achieving a goal. It complements and enhances decision and focus by spinning the lock and revealing new combinations and ways of helping you to achieve the goal.

Let's face it … your goal is going to end in one of three conditions:

VICTORY or **WATERED DOWN** or **FAILURE**

Planning is the key tool that helps you to significantly increase the probability of success.

Go into each new endeavor with your eyes open and a good plan in hand along with the support that comes from obeying **RULE #5 … INVOLVE OTHERS!**

#5

INVOLVE OTHERS

Success leaves clues and here's an important one: No matter who you are, where you live, what your goal is, somebody has already been there and done that.

There are no new battles. History repeats itself; all goals—from soup to nuts—have been attempted and achieved or attempted and failed by others!

You can earn good judgment and knowledge the old-fashioned way—through the school of hard knocks—or you can reach out, tap into experience, and make significant performance improvements. The choice is up to you.

It is your prime responsibility to acquire useful knowledge from others and to apply it appropriately. You don't have to reinvent the wheel, but you do have to learn from those who did.

Effective goal setting is consultative; it doesn't squander, it leverages all available brainpower. Welcome and actively seek multiple perspectives on any given problem.

It behooves you to do your homework, to read, and to converse with others who have first-hand knowledge based on actual experience. Shortening your learning curve saves buckets of blood, sweat, tears, time, and money.

EXPERIENCE IS THE MOTHER'S MILK OF A SUCCESSFUL GOAL. THE BENEFIT OF INVOLVING OTHERS IN YOUR PLANS IS YOUR ACCESSIBILITY TO EXPERIENCE, KNOWLEDGE, AND WISDOM.

There will come a time when you will be unsure; that's why having another set of eyes and ears is essential. There can't be enough said about the importance of intellectual bench strength.

The only meaningful way to evaluate an individual and his or her methods is by looking at results. From raising good children to investing for retirement, from maintaining excellent health to spiritual peace … others have already made the trip. Search them out, and learn from what they did both right and wrong.

As you pursue a goal, knowledge is your greatest ally. With it you advance, without it you stumble. Progress is dependent upon momentum, and momentum is dependent upon information that advances you closer to victory.

Useful knowledge obtained from others' experiences allows you to build and maintain momentum. Trying to achieve a goal without obtaining knowledge from others is a recipe for false starts and performance hiccups.

Goals mean growth, and growth requires new knowledge. Purposely, systematically solicit and import useful information. How? Read books, ask questions, attend seminars, observe … pay attention. Teachers are everywhere, both living and dead, among strangers and friends alike.

No goal is achieved in a vacuum. We all need the guidance and support that comes only from involving others. Progress improves in direct proportion to the quality of your knowledge. Lack of knowledge invites fear, intimidation, and hesitation.

GOOD, SOLID, PROVEN KNOWLEDGE AND EXPERIENCE INSPIRE CONFIDENCE AND ACTION. YOU MUST SURROUND YOURSELF WITH GOOD PEOPLE WHO POSSESS SOLID EXPERIENCE.

It is possible to get decades of knowledge in days if you do two things: Believe it is possible, and surround yourself with knowledgeable people.

Choose a mentor or build a personal board of directors, a handpicked cast of characters that will help you craft a brilliant performance. Your weaknesses can become strengths. What your mentor or board of directors knows is worth knowing.

Take your promising ideas to people you trust and let them help you with perspective, talent, money, etc. Welcome prompt observations, detailed evaluations and even ruthless critiques of your plans.

Value experience above all else. Acquire it actively for yourself. Seek it out in others.

You involve others for their vision and experience. Your purpose must be to have them help you remove or manage as many unnecessary barriers that exist.

IN ADDITION TO SHORTENING YOUR LEARNING CURVE, INVOLVING OTHERS IN YOUR GOAL PROVIDES AN ADDITIONAL LEVEL OF ACCOUNTABILITY WHICH IS MANDATORY FOR SUCCESS.

And when Murphy's Law presents itself and your best-laid plans unravel, a well-chosen group of confidants can help you to understand the wisdom of RULE #6 ... WELCOME FAILURE!

FIRST SAY TO YOURSELF WHAT YOU WOULD BE; AND THEN DO WHAT YOU HAVE TO DO.

— Epictetus

#6

WELCOME FAILURE

The dreaded "F" word—failure—is so important yet so misunderstood. The key to understanding how to succeed rests on knowing a thing or two about the importance of failure.

FAILURE
IS BOTH THE "TEACHER'S PET" AND THE "BLACK SHEEP" OF THE FAMILY OF SUCCESS!

People are naive about the benefits of failure. Wrongly founded assumptions about failure replace potentially accurate assessments of what is necessary to achieve success.

Failure, which spends much of its life in the gulag of public perception, is, by all measures, essential to success. It is failure's peculiar fate that its reputation is routinely reinforced by negative perceptions.

FAILURE HAS AN ULTERIOR MOTIVE … not to get you to quit, but to stop you long enough so that you may learn something, re-strategize, and re-launch again more prepared for success.

Success cannot exist without failure as failure is part of the steering mechanism that drives you to success. Learn to expect failure—welcome it, as your denial of this reality can and will have huge negative effects.

Anything worthwhile is worth pursuing, even though the risk is huge, the investment formidable, and failure a possibility.

✗ FAILURE is an essential part of the combination required to open the lock on success.

✗ FAILURE measures your personal investment in this goal—it is a test of character, commitment, and courage.

✗ FAILURE lobs an occasional grenade at success, failure asks for your resignation letter, it goads and prods you into quitting, but success hangs in the balance.

We all live a life of close calls, belly flops, and missed opportunities. The truth is we're all cowards, some are just bigger cowards than others. Your persistence in the face of failure and set back is a measure of your belief in yourself and your goal.

HELLO
MY GOAL IS

to learn from my
Failures

Knowing when to say when is also important. The message this time could be to say "Uncle" and move on to something else. An occasional step back to regroup and reload can, and often does, position you for several more steps forward.

There will always be tension between your enthusiasm for your goal and the fear of failing to achieve it. Quite frankly, you want it that way. The trick is learning how not to surrender to fear but to thrive on its tension.

EXPECT TO GET DINGED HERE AND THERE AS YOU PURSUE YOUR GOAL, BUT LIKE WINE THAT GETS BETTER WITH AGE, YOU GET BETTER WHEN YOU HAVE FAILED A TIME OR TWO AND LEARNED FROM THE EXPERIENCE.

While there is nothing inherently sexy or enviable about failure, eventually people find you more attractive and interesting because of the knowledge, wisdom, and maturity you gained because of it.

When opportunity appears on the horizon, fear of failure is often riding shotgun. Too many people surrender to that fear. Stay focused, "super glue" your commitment, and persevere.

I KNOW THE PRICE
OF SUCCESS: DEDICATION,
HARD WORK, AND AN
UNREMITTING DEVOTION
TO THE THINGS YOU WANT
TO SEE HAPPEN.

— *Frank Lloyd Wright*

Your reward is having a wonderful stage upon which to ply your craft, to explore yourself, and to let the world enjoy the benefits of your efforts.

Failure does not preclude success. Rather than beat a retreat, go on the offensive; dare to pursue your dreams when others would yield.

Failure is a form of turbulence. It serves as a wake up call that challenges you to get ready, get set, and go for **RULE #7 ... TAKE PURPOSEFUL ACTION!**

#7

TAKE PURPOSEFUL ACTION

The odds that you'll succeed without taking action are about the same as winning the lottery without buying a ticket!

For those times when you feel trapped, stressed, or in a prison

of your own making, take purposeful action. It's your Get-Out-Of-Jail-Free card.

In real estate it's location, location, location. In goal-setting it's

ACTION, ACTION, ACTION.

You can't just stick out your thumb and hitchhike your way to success, you've got to roll up your sleeves and do the work that needs to be done.

Be seduced by the attractiveness of your goal. Inaction leads to impotence. Taking purposeful action immunizes you from "Goal Parkinson's," a long, slow goodbye to your dreams, talents and destiny.

A quality life is accomplished when thoughtful attention, goal setting, and purposeful action click into position. Whether your dream is to be or not to be is largely dependent upon your actions.

The cure for the ills of procrastination is a heavy prescription of action, until the day arrives when your dreams and their achievement are one in the same. When that day arrives, dream bigger dreams and take more action.

A good plan will almost always get you in the door, but it is action that seals the deal. So you want a guarantee? Well here it is:

WITHOUT PURPOSEFUL ACTION, THE ONLY GUARANTEE IS FAILURE AND MEDIOCRITY!

Maximum productivity is working economically. It is managing time and resources effectively. You need to know when to move – and to know when to rest and to prepare to move.

Don't tiptoe toward your goal, walk confidently before it waltzes off into the arms of neglect. Dreams become reality through one simple mode of transportation: purposeful action.

The continuation of bad habits, such as procrastination and poor follow through, is like having an addiction to weapons of mass destruction.

It is tragically un-hip to procrastinate. Unfortunately, the vast majority of people never display their true potential; it never has an opening night … never makes a debut.

The bulk of potential resides deep within each individual just waiting to come out, and it stays there because people are afraid.

The mechanics of achieving a goal make it easy for people to relate to the necessity of action. But when action is not purposeful, it can be an Achilles heel.

When we operate without planning, we remain forever scattered and confused. You're always busy, but not much gets accomplished. Without a deeper appreciation and application of planning, the most you can expect is marginal improvement.

Intimidate your fears through purposeful goal-directed activity. Since when is being the underdog any reason for not pursuing your dreams? Remember, it's not the size of the dog in the fight … it's the size of the fight in the dog!

 DON'T JUST PURSUE YOUR GOAL … INHABIT IT. WEAR IT, ACT IT, LIVE IT, TASTE IT! GET COMMITTED—TAKE ACTION. LIFE IS NOT A SCRATCH-AND-SNIFF TEST!

When you set a goal, there's distance between your current reality and desired reality. Procrastination increases the distance and minimizes the chances of achievement. Procrastination is the mother of regret. It postpones the future, aborts liftoff at the last minute.

Unless you take action to achieve your goals, life becomes a constant series of postponements, cancel-lations, and missed opportunities.

You will never attain your goals simply by thinking and talking about them. You must take action as all sucess comes down to execution.

Now that purposeful action is in and procrastination is out, ensure your success with **RULE #8 ... INSPECT WHAT YOU EXPECT!**

I KNOW THAT I HAVE THE
ABILITY TO ACHIEVE THE OBJECT
OF MY DEFINITE PURPOSE
IN LIFE, THEREFORE, I DEMAND OF
MYSELF PERSISTENT, CONTINUOUS
ACTION TOWARD ITS ATTAINMENT,
AND I HERE AND NOW PROMISE
TO RENDER SUCH ACTION.

—*Napoleon Hill*

#8

INSPECT
WHAT YOU EXPECT

CHANGE IS INEVITABLE—GROWTH IS OPTIONAL. Change knocks the wind out of all good plans. Unless performance is reviewed regularly, growth becomes stunted.

We get what we inspect, not just what we expect.

ATTENTION INCREASES PRODUCTIVITY!

Be uncompromising in areas that permit no compromises, such as inspecting your expectations. Do not hesitate to evaluate your progress. If you believe that taking time to inspect your expectations is incompatible with progress, rethink your definition of progress.

Inspection actually expands time by helping to maintain focus. If you do not use time properly through regular inspections, you burn it through neglect.

Just as DNA's coding is built into every cell of your body, the combination for achieving any goal requires the inspection of expectations.

INSPECTION HAS A DUAL PURPOSE:

FIRST, INSPECTION TELLS YOU WHERE YOU ARE IN RELATION TO WHERE YOU WANT TO BE.

SECOND, IT TELLS YOU HOW YOU ARE DOING IN THE PROCESS OF PURSUING YOUR GOALS.

You must evaluate whether the actions you are taking are going to produce the results you desire. It is important to perpetuate and amplify those actions that produce desired results.

You are your own judge, jury, and executioner when it comes to evaluating a goal and deciding what action to take, whether it be changing tactics or dropping the goal.

When you know for certain that you are on the wrong road, you change course. But if you are driving along ignoring landmarks and road signs, you may continue on the wrong road for a long time without knowing you are lost.

YOU WILL MAKE PROGRESS WHEN YOU TAKE TIME TO INSPECT PAST PERFORMANCE AND LEARN FROM YOUR EXPERIENCE.

The purpose of measuring performance and inspecting expectations is to improve performance. You must know how you are performing the "must do" actions necessary to achieve your goals. Inspecting expectations allows you to know what you are looking for before you actually see it!

inspect

The best time to establish expectations is when you establish your overall plan. That way you can evaluate the tasks before you act, prepare mentally, and set a pace.

Start off knowing the rules, and how you must play to succeed. Inspections are meant to revisit, revise and reinforce predetermined standards of performance.

Inspecting expectations confirms that time and efforts are productive in achieving the intended results. You need to ensure that what you want done gets done!

An inspection process will make you aware of performance gaps. It is this "white space" that you must manage to achieve the results you desire.

Look at this as a personal performance audit or balance sheet that quickly informs you of your assets and liabilities. You will undoubtedly see and feel changes in your life; they will be distinct and noticeable when you inspect your expectations.

NO plan holds up against the weight of opposition and adversity. The shelf life of any plan expires quickly if it is not reviewed and updated. Good intentions, while honorable, are of little use when you let years of potential and possibility slip by uninspected.

The old adage "Don't expect if you don't inspect" holds true in setting and achieving a goal. Many serious problems begin with small items that go unnoticed by the untrained and undisciplined eye. Changing them early is a low-maintenance activity, if left unattended they can require a major overhaul.

One last thing to consider, if you don't inspect your progress and results, how will you know when you deserve a good pat on the back for a job well done?

Expecting a reward for goals achieved is what you will learn from **RULE #9 ... REWARD YOURSELF!**

IF YOU CAN'T MEASURE IT, YOU CAN'T MANAGE IT.

— Unknown

71

#9

REWARD YOURSELF

A funny thing happens on the way to success: You build integrity, character, heart, discipline, and a host of other intrinsic benefits that add credence to the old saying, **"THE JOURNEY IS ITS OWN REWARD."**

GOALS ARE GENERATORS OF
VALUE,
OFTEN BECAUSE OF WHAT YOU LEARNED AND BECAME EN ROUTE.

But having something that symbolizes achievement—a reward— is a powerful extrinsic motivator for continued progress.

Pre-flight instructions always inform you to put on your own oxygen mask before attempting to help others. That's because we can't possibly help others until our own needs are met.

If your "flight" is the pursuit of a goal, one of your basic needs is the need for appreciation. And the best

Recognition celebrates achievement and builds confidence; it provides an incentive to further achievement. It is an indispensable self-management tool.

person to meet that need is the one looking back at you in the mirror. **MAKE REWARDING YOURSELF STANDARD PROTOCOL!**

Imagine all the effort a new lover takes to get your attention … flowers, chocolates, a song dedicated to you broadcast from your favorite radio station, a surprise call or personalized card that tells you how special you are.

How long has it been since you've paid yourself such consideration?

WE NEED REWARDS TO GIVE OURSELVES ENCOURAGEMENT AND TO REMIND US THAT WE HAVE ACHIEVED IMPORTANT GOALS.

Don't let your achievement and the feeling of victory evaporate without some kind of reward and recognition. Rewarding yourself for your accomplishments is an essential part of the combination for success.

A war hero may receive a Purple Heart, Bronze Star, or Congressional Medal of Honor. These awards remind the holders, their families, and the world community of acts of courage, bravery, and selflessness.

Rewards continue to inspire long after specific accomplishments fade from memory!

After all, you probably kick yourself when you screw up. Why not pat yourself on the back when you achieve your goal. Be proud of your accomplishments!

RECOGNIZE YOUR OWN ACHIEVEMENT.

There can't be enough said of having earned something and enjoying the fruits of your labor.

The best predictor of future behavior is past behavior, and when you reward the right behavior and results, you almost guarantee a repeat performance.

Rewards are good positive reinforcements—they make you feel good about your achievements, and they reinforce the behavior and attitudes that led to those achievements. The range of rewards is great.

Here are a few principles of rewarding yourself:

- *Always reward your major achievements.*
- *Reward yourself for intermediate steps and victories.*
- *Make rewards commensurate with the accomplishment.*
- *Ensure that rewards are personal and sentimental.*

A reward provides an effective but uncomplicated means for reinforcing the actions most important to success. Rewards are reminders of your potential for success.

You should reward yourself for small accomplishments as well as large; this simple act becomes fuel for future achievement!

3 Cs
OF ACHIEVING
GOALS

=

Commitment
Concentration
Courage

A goal, once achieved, is the poster child of commitment, concentration, and courage. It deserves to be rewarded!

Your succession plan from one goal to the next should include both celebration and introspection. However, to enjoy those celebrations, you need the commitment that comes only from **RULE #10 ... MAINTAIN PERSONAL INTEGRITY!**

YOU GET WHAT YOU REWARD. BE CLEAR ABOUT WHAT YOU WANT TO GET AND SYSTEMAT- ICALLY REWARD IT.

— Bob Nelson

#10

MAINTAIN PERSONAL INTEGRITY

What's the point of setting a goal if you have no intention of ever achieving it?

You've come too far to give up now. Personal integrity is the

integrity

final spin of the dial, the one that springs the lock and allows you to swing open the vault of success!

It's personal integrity that fundamentally unites the other nine rules.

YOUR BIGGEST CONCERN IS NOT YOUR SKILL, ABILITY, OR INTELLIGENCE— IT'S YOUR COMMITMENT.

Unless you are committed, there will be a sense of negligence to everything you do. The "Promised Land" is for those who exercise personal integrity. Personal integrity means maintaining a commitment to your commitment. It's about setting a goal and keeping your promise to achieve it … end of story!

Personal integrity is what achievement is all about. The moments you feel like quitting are the times you must take a flashlight to your soul and inspect yourself for will, courage, and spirit.

Don't tarnish your goal by doing something so bush league as quitting just because things got difficult.

Lack of integrity ensures false promises and broken dreams; it negatively reinforces a sense of incompetence. Failure to honor your commitments to yourself is the biggest mistake you can make; it reflects an absolute disregard for the sanctity of your own goal.

Saturate your goal with a heavy dose of personal integrity. Without it, your goal becomes more whim than vision, more a scheme than a dream. Lack of personal integrity is like a slow leak in a tire ...

> values lay the groundwork for your goals; goals lead to the fulfillment of your mission; your mission leads to the realization of your life's work – your legacy.

eventually everything goes flat.

If success is your destination, you will arrive there on a carriage called Planning pulled by a horse named Integrity.

Commitments are easier to make than to meet. But the joke is on you if you think you can achieve a goal—any goal—without commitment. You are called on to fulfill your promises. A large part of your success will come from sheer tenacity!

What's at stake at this stage is profoundly more important than the goal itself. Hanging in the balance is the essence of your life … your character and overall success. You simply can't afford to quit!

Personal integrity builds intellectual and psychological muscle. Yet, many people have the psychological strength of a "98-pound weakling."

You make yourself vulnerable to failure every time you exercise cream puff ethics. You deprive yourself the company of success and the fruits of your efforts by quitting.

Personal integrity is the countdown clock of your goal. It starts ticking the second you begin and stops when you achieve the goal or quit.

Without personal integrity, you can say, "Farewell dream. Adios potential. Toodleloo success. Hello mediocrity!" Your goal will find a more deserving soul … someone with courage, character, and conviction. Someone who keeps promises!

Personal integrity is not only habitual but also essential—it moves you ever closer to your goal and ultimate success.

Commitment is the heartbeat of your goal. In order to keep your goal breathing, rely on the oxygen of integrity.

GO AHEAD, TOUCH THAT DIAL. TURN TO PERSONAL INTEGRITY TO KEEP YOUR DREAM ALIVE AND TO PROVIDE THE STAYING POWER NEEDED TO CROSS THE FINISH LINE TO ACHIEVEMENT!

REVIEWING THE

10

RULES

TO ACHIEVING SUCCESS

#1 BE DECISIVE

The difference between what one person and another achieves depends more on goal choices than on abilities. The profound differences between successful people and others are the goals they choose to pursue. Individuals with similar talents, intelligence, and abilities will achieve different results because they select and pursue different goals.

#2 STAY FOCUSED

Focus creates a powerful force: goal power. The moment you focus on a goal, your goal becomes a magnet, pulling you and your resources toward it. The more focused your energies, the more power you generate. There is a seismic shift in performance that takes place when you move from decisiveness to focus.

#3 WRITE YOUR GOALS

When you write a goal, you actually see what you're thinking. You have a target to aim for … something that takes shape and grows legs. By writing your goals, you take a step toward achieving them. Goals not written down fall victim to the "out of sight … out of mind" phenomenon!

#4 PLAN THOROUGHLY

You can virtually guarantee your success in any endeavor if you know who you are, what you want, where you are going, how you will get there, and what you will do once you arrive. Planning before you act helps you to do things better, faster, and cheaper!

#5 INVOLVE OTHERS

It is your prime responsibility to acquire useful knowledge from others and to apply it appropriately. You don't have to reinvent the wheel. It behooves you to do your homework, to read, and to converse with others who have first-hand knowledge based on actual experience. Shortening your learning curve saves buckets of blood, sweat, tears, time, and money.

#6 WELCOME FAILURE

People are naive about the benefits of failure. Wrongly founded assumptions about failure replace potentially accurate assessments of what is necessary to achieve success. Failure, which spends much of its life in the gulag of public perception, is essential to success.

#7 TAKE PURPOSEFUL ACTION

In real estate it's location, location, location. In goal-setting its action, action, action! You can't just stick out your thumb and hitchhike your way to success. You've got to roll up your sleeves and do the work that needs to be done. The acid test of goal setting is purposeful action.

#8 INSPECT WHAT YOU EXPECT

The purpose of measuring performance and inspecting expectations is to improve performance. You must know how you are performing the "must do" actions necessary to achieve your goals. Inspecting expectations allows you to know what you are looking for before you actually see it!

#9 REWARD YOURSELF

A goal, once achieved, symbolizes commitment, concentration, and courage, and it deserves to be rewarded. A reward provides an effective but uncomplicated means of reinforcing the actions most important to success. Rewards are reminders of our potential for achievement. We should reward ourselves daily for small accomplishments; this simple act becomes fuel for future achievement.

#10 MAINTAIN PERSONAL INTEGRITY

Personal integrity is the countdown clock of your goal. It starts ticking the second you begin and stops when you achieve the goal or quit. The "Promised Land" is for those who exercise personal integrity. Personal integrity means maintaining a commitment to your commitment. It's about setting a goal and keeping your promise to achieve it ... end of story!

A FINAL THOUGHT!

Successful people …

❌ Cannot be vague or ambiguous;

they must decide what is wanted!

❌ Remain focused from beginning to end!

❌ Realize that writing down all goals adds

clarity, depth, and objectivity!

❌ Are master planners. They create the necessary

strategy to achieve their goals!

❌ Realize that no one goes through life alone and

that their successes are largely dependent on the

people with whom they surround themselves!

❌ Understand that failure is part of the equation

that leads to success!

✖ Understand there is a time for planning and a time for action, and they take purposeful action because only action produces results!

✖ Appreciate the value of progress checks and regular inspections!

✖ Reward themselves for their efforts.

✖ Applaud their hard work and sacrifices and enjoy the success they sought and created!

✖ Keep their promises; their resolve is firm, deliberate, and in place until the goal is achieved!

SUCCESSFUL PEOPLE SUCCEED BECAUSE THEY WORK
THE ENTIRE COMBINATION—ALL TEN RULES—TO TURN

DREAMS INTO REALITY!

GARY RYAN BLAIR has been called one of the world ' s most influential thinkers on excellence and productivity and has been a keynote speaker and facilitator for such organizations as IBM, Federal Express, Subway, and the U.S. Army, and he conducts workshops for individuals and organizations around the world.

He is the president of The GoalsGuy and has more than 20 years of experience helping business owners, corporate executives, and sales professionals manage their time, set their priorities, and stay focused so they can achieve their goals, grow their business, and build sustainable competitive advantage.

His work has been featured in the *New York Times*, the *Wall Street Journal*, *USA Today*, *Rolling Stone*, and many other publications. He is a dynamic and entertaining speaker who makes the heart sing, the mind expand, and the spirit soar.

He can be reached for speaking engagements at:

PHONE: 1.877.462.5748
EMAIL: Info@GoalsGuy.com
WEB: www.EverythingCounts.com

If you have enjoyed this book we invite you to check out our entire collection of gift books, with free inspirational movies, at **www.simpletruths.com.** You'll discover it's a great way to inspire **friends** and **family,** or to thank your best **customers** and **employees.**

The
simple truths®
DIFFERENCE

212°
SERVIC
THE **10** RULES FOR CREATING A SERVICE

BY MAC AN

LEADING WITH
PASSION
10 ESSENTIALS *for* INSPIRING OTHERS

JOHN J. MURPHY

For more information, please visit us at:
www.simpletruths.com
Or call us toll free… 800-900-3427